THOMAS MATHEWSON'S 1805 FENCING FAMILIARISED

A transcription with commentary and notes on its use in Historical Fencing.

Acknowledgements have to be made to Mike and Nick Thomas for providing the copies of Hutton's works and to them and other members of the Academy of Historic Fencing on whom many of these moves have been tried out.

(c) 2009 Tim Jones

All rights reserved

No part of this publication may be produced, stored in a retrieval system, or transmitted in any form or by any means, without the prior permission in writing of the publisher, nor be otherwise circulated in any form of binding or cover other than in which it is published and without a similar condition including this condition being imposed on the subsequent purchaser.

First published in Great Britain by Swordworks Books

ISBN 978-1906512323

Printed and bound in the UK & US

A catalogue record of this book is available from the British Library

Cover design by Swordworks Books

Table of Contents

INTRODUCTION 6
PART I: TRANSCRIPTION 8
   CHAPTER I OF THE DRAWING AND HOLDING THE SWORD. 14
   CHAPTER II-OF THE FIGURE OF EIGHT DOWNWARDS AND UPWARDS. 15
   CHAPTER III-OF THE INSIDE GUARD. 16
   CHAPTER IV-OF THE OUTSIDE GUARD. 17
   CHAPTER V-OF THE MEDIUM GUARD. 19
   CHAPTER VI-OF THE HANGING GUARD. 20
   CHAPTER VII-OF THE FOUR GUARDS, LEFT FOOT STANDING. 21
   CHAPTER VIII-OF THE FOUR GUARDS, TRAVERSING TO THE LEFT AND RIGHT. 22
   CHAPTER IX-OF THE FOUR GUARDS, ADVANCING AND RETREATING. 23
   CHAPTER X-OF THROWING AT THE HEAD AND SLIPPING THE LEG. 25
   CHAPTER XI-OF THE SCHOLAR'S DEFENSIVE. 26
   CHAPTER XII-OF THE SCHOLAR'S OFFENSIVE. 28
   CHAPTER XII-OF THE SALUTE. 32
   CHAPTER XIV-OF PLAYING LOOSE. 33
   CHAPTER XV- OF HOW YOU ARE TO ACT OFFENSIVELY. 36
   CHAPTER XVI- OF HOW YOU ARE TO ACT DEFENSIVELY. 37
   CHAPTER XVII- OF DISARMING. 38
   CHAPTER XVIII- OF PREVENTING DISARMS. 39
   CHAPTER XIX- OF THE BEATING OF THE SWORD. 40
   CHAPTER XX- OF THE GLIZADE. 41
   CHAPTER XXI- OF LEFT-HANDED PLAYERS. 42
   CHAPTER XXII- OF THRUSTING. 43
   CHAPTER XXIII- OF JUDGEMENT. 44
PART II: SWORD VERSUS BAYONET OR SPEAR 45
PART III: TRAINING 51
   STANCES 56
GLOSSARY 67
REFERENCES 71
APPENDIX I 73

Introduction.

It is my intention with this new edition of Mathewson's work to produce a manual that will be useful to those wishing to recreate the training regime of one particular fencing master from the reign of George III. This particular manual is of relevance and use because it seems to have been written with the intention of offering instruction at varying levels starting with the complete beginner and is therefore, unlike many earlier manuals and indeed some contemporary ones, suitable for those modern fencing masters who have recruits to teach. One envisages it as being of value to three categories of people, as well as hopefully being of interest to those with a more general interest in the history of fencing. Firstly to those within the Western Martial Arts community who may wish to study a different master's works from the earlier ones that seem to be the most commonly followed. Secondly I hope it will be of value to those re-enactors who portray the late eighteenth and early nineteenth century enabling them to produce a more authentic representation of sword work of that period and for displays away from the battlefield I particularly draw their attention to the drill en masse as presented in appendix 1 which would make an interesting display in those circumstances where fighting may not be appropriate. Finally, this work may be of some value to those staging theatrical events in that it gives these a grounding of correct sword moves and postures. Indeed to all the foregoing the particular value of this work is that it draws attention to the differences between sword drill as taught and practised in the Napoleonic period and the modern versions of it that are based, as is modern sport sabre, on the late Victorian sabre drill as exemplified by Alfred Hutton's works.

To set this work in the context of its time the period between 1802 and Nelson's victory at Trafalgar saw Britain in the grip of an invasion scare that resulted in numerous measures, both governmental and private, to put the country in a state of readiness to receive the French should they land. It is against this background that Mathewson's manual should be set. This may provide the explanation for certain features within it. Although Mathewson describes it as being about the "Scotch Broad Sword" it is obvious from his work that he meant it to apply to all similar cut and thrust weapons, something that may have been necessary given the need to equip a large number of volunteers raised against this eventuality which would, of necessity, have entailed the reuse of older arms, although theoretically the cavalry volunteers should all have been equipped with the 1796 pattern light cavalry sabre (Mileham, 1983, 6). This does however, have the happy side effect for us of increasing the range of weapons for which this manual may be used even beyond the wide range used to illustrate the original work.

Part I: Transcription[1]

To the volunteers of the United Kingdom of Great Britain.

At a crisis so important as the present, unparalleled in the annals of our history[2], permit me to address a work to your notice, which combines the principles of an art that cannot fail, if studied with any tolerable attention and care, securing to us the preservation of those rights and liberties, which have for ages rendered our country the emporium of every thing dear and valuable in civilised life.

Yes, valiant defenders of our country, permit one who has long combated the perils of a military life, (with how much honour he shall leave his fellow soldiers to say) and has devoted the better part of his years, in attaining the practical and theoretical knowledge of Self-Defence; as an humble Veteran, suffer him to offer the Fruits of his Labours on 'the sacred Altar of his Country;' convinced that he cannot present them to a more loyal, patriotic , and brave people, than those he now has the honour to address.

T. Mathewson.

Salford, Manchester, February 23rd, 1805.

Advertisement.

To my *scholars*,

The encouragement which you have so kindly given me, and the success I have met with since my commencement as a Teacher in Manchester, embolden me to present you with a Treatise on the Broad

---

[1] Transcriber's note: for the most part I have attempted to faithfully reproduce Mathewson's original text with a minimum of modernised spellings. However, I have made additions in three areas; firstly I have altered the use of italicised letters for clarity and in the following the reader should note that where a word is in italics it is to be found in the glossary and on a related note I have highlighted in bold particularly important statements; secondly the footnotes are of course my own not Mathewson's. finally the illustrations have been modified for clarity missing out accoutrements such as scabbards.

[2] This work was published before Nelson's victory at Trafalgar relieved much of the fear of invasion and caused the militias to be stood down (Owen, 1990, 46).

Sword[3], manifesting the superiority of that weapon, over a spear, Pike, or Gun and Bayonet[4], in the hope that it will be esteemed a mark of my grateful acknowledgement, for the honour I received in your choice of me as a *Master*, as well as for the further confidence you have placed in me, and so fully testified by your generous recommendations, motives of weight sufficient to awaken all my zeal; the more we are indebted to the exercise of any art, the greater is the obligation we lie under of endeavouring to carry it to its highest perfection; a consideration which must necessarily stimulate me to exert my utmost efforts, both in order to answer the expectations of my *Scholars*; and to discharge that duty which I owe to myself.

The principles laid down in the following Treatise are such as have arisen from the most serious and elaborate attention of thirty years practice, in most of the principal cities and towns in Great Britain and Ireland: being thirty years in His Majesty's service, I made it my study to find out and frequent the company of the most able swordsmen and *masters*, in order to draw instructions from hearing them discuss, and examine all cuts and guards; I found their aim always was to simplify the *play*[5] in order to render it the more certain.

The undernamed swordsmen and teachers I have had the honour of being intimately acquainted with, viz.

Captain and Adjutant, Richardson, 3rd Dragoons.

---

[3] Despite this the plates used by Mathewson indicate that he did not restrict his system to the broad sword let alone the 'Scotch' variety but included the *spadroon* and a number of infantry officer's swords. Interestingly he does not seem to have included the then current service swords in his illustrations despite the 1788 ordinance requiring officers to carry the same swords as their men (Robson, 1996, 74) equally interesting is that despite his association with the 3rd Dragoons he does not seem to include any heavy cavalry swords. Mathewson does however seem fond of illustrating the curved swords of the light cavalry which suggests this manual may have been intended for the yeomanry and fencibles who carried these swords (Mileham, 1983, 6) and were enthusiastic proponents of fencing training (Mileham, 1983, 11). This may also explain the use of the spadroon since paintings of Sir Martin Bourne Ffolkes, Bart., from 1783 and Sir William Skeffington, Bart., from 1794 (Smitherman, 1967, plates I and II) suggest that such straighter swords may have been preferred by some yeomanry officers.

[4] As Hutton (1889, 135) noted this claim, that dates back to at least 1628 (Thibault cited by Wise, 1971, 122, 124-5), needs to be taken with caution since it only applies if the 'spearman' is significantly less competent with his weapon than the swordsman.

[5] Although Hutton (1889, 1) thought this had gone too far, as an introduction to fencing it is a sound principle.

Lieutenant and Adjutant Lascelles, 3rd Dragoons.

Serjeant Milley, 3rd Dragoons.

Serjeant Walker, 3rd Dragoons.

James Craven, 3rd Dragoons.

John Newhouse, 3rd Dragoons.

Quarter-master Stanley, 3rd Dragoon Guards.

Mr Parks, late Life Guards.

Adjutant Malcolm, 2nd Dragoons.

Serjeant Angus, 2nd Dragoons.

George Penn, 2nd Dragoons.

James Crage, 2nd Dragoons.

Serjeant-major Phillips, 2nd Dragoon Guards.

Serjeant Benson, 7th Dragoons.

Mr Bell, 10th Dragoons.

Serjeant Chapman, 15th Dragoons.

Serjeant-major Grant, 42nd Foot.

Mr Campbell, Teacher, Glasgow.

Mr Pearson, Teacher, Dublin.

Mr McGregor Teacher, Paisley.

Mr Rogerson, Teacher, Edinburgh.

Mr McLane, Teacher, Galloway.

I shall esteem myself happy, if in all my endeavours, I am enabled to demonstrate the ardent desire I have to render the art, of which I am a professor, at once both useful and agreeable.

In order to attain both these ends, there can be no other method adopted than that of a theory well founded. Such as may serve as a basis to all those movements which an agile and well framed body is capable of practising, in order thereby to discover their defects, or to point out their particular merit; without theory nothing satisfactory can be expected[6], nor is it possible to act with judgement, for it must not be imagined, that that to acquire some general notions by mere dint of practice is sufficient: this is only the bare outline of the art, and leaves the subject untouched; the essence of it is to draw a progressive system of instructions from one cut to another[7], and when to use it with advantage; this is what I have endeavoured in the best manner I could demonstrate to you; how far I have succeeded, I submit to your determination.

Introduction.

This treatise will, I hope, be well received by the lovers of fencing; the perusal of it from time to time must also serve to recall the principles to mind, and enable the reader to arrive as near perfection as possible; for it is not enough to preserve equality as an exercise, and to practise it now and then; the memory must be refreshed by frequent revisals and by frequent examination of the principles; theory being as necessary as practice.

I have expressed myself in as clear and intelligible a manner as I am able, in order to be understood even by those who have not learnt this art; I have also put the necessary plates to establish and elucidate the principal guards and cuts of this art.

I would not add any more, because those who follow may take their origin from the principles explained in this treatise; neither do I speak of the *St George's guard, half hanging guard*, and others, which

---

[6] Not necessarily a uniformly popular sentiment, then or now.

[7] Nowhere is this approach clearer than in the exercise en masse presented here as appendix 1.

are found obstructive to the proficiency of the learner, and which the ancients used only for ineffectual show[8], and to lengthen their lessons[9].

It may be found in History the art of fencing has been practised by our forefathers, and we find that in the West of England Magistrates encourage it to this day[10]; and the Edinburgh Highland Society gives prizes for both *Masters* and *scholars*- for this art ought to be regarded as one of the most useful, since its sole object is the defence of honour and of our country[11]; it is at the same time the most noble, as it makes a part or rather the basis of military exercises[12]; it is the duty of every *master* to endeavour to improve upon his profession, and contribute to carrying it to perfection; this exercise is a defence more or les secure; and this defence proceeds from the principles we use; it is those that determine the danger; it is those that constitute the security; this security equally consists in all the cuts and *thrusts*[13], but it depends on one only: the point of greater consequence is to throw it just, and according to the principles; it is not the having attained even some eminence in the practical knowledge of an art, by the long and continued exercise of it, that can enable a *master* to convey proper instructions; it is the ground and principles of it that must be scientifically known, and to form himself by it in order to make his lessons clear and instructive, and form his pupils with judgement and dispatch: nothing being more evident than that it is a much greater task to teach than to exercise any art; it is the cultivation of this art that unfetters the body, strengthens it and makes it upright; it is it that gives a becoming deportment and an easy carriage,

---

[8] A point of view criticised by Alfred Hutton (1889, 1) who thought that nineteenth century military fencers had been too quick to simplify and as a result he believed fencing had regressed not improved.

[9] This is not necessarily a bad thing if Wise (1971, 53) is correct that the complexity of the Spanish system meant its practitioners spent so long learning it that inevitably they became better fighters.

[10] Castle (1885, 210) thought this had ceased in the first quarter of the nineteenth century and was even then restricted to "some old-fashioned parts of England" while Hutton (1901, 347) thought it continued to mid century.

[11] An interesting point given that Edward I in 1285 banned fencing schools from London since it encouraged misbehaviour (Brown, 1997, 17).

[12] Given the essentially individualistic nature of swordplay this is questionable.

[13] Despite this Mathewson largely ignores the thrusts.

activity and agility, grace and dignity;-it is it that opportunely awes petulance[14], softens and polishes savageness and rudeness, and animates a proper confidence;-it is it which in teaching us to conquer ourselves, that we may be able to conquer others, imprints respect, and gives true valour, good nature and politeness; *in fine*, which makes a man fit for society[15]:-Therefore it is not only necessary to youth, by its contributing to form the constitution-it is besides an accomplishment of education. Every exercise in general has its advantage, and concurs in accomplishing one general effect-but none more so than fencing can give ease and freedom, because in it every part of the body is continually in action; and, to crown all, it brings and confirms health, than which no blessing is more desirable; *in fine*, it has, among others, two inseparable qualities, the agreeable and the useful;-the former, as it affords gentlemen a noble and distinguished amusement-the latter, as it forms the body, and furnishes them with the faculty of defence[16], whether it be of their honour or of their life, when one or the other finds itself brought in question by disagreeable accident, or attacked by those turbulent and dangerous persons, whose correction is often of service to society in general.

---

[14] Without naming names any reader who has entered a modern sport fencing competition particularly in foil may be excused a moment of incredulity at this claim.

[15] This exhortation alone is worth transcribing this work for and, like most martial arts, gives added reason to study what by some is derided as impractical and outmoded.

[16] This remark is of course of little relevance today when for those so interested there are far more practical forms of self defence available than the techniques presented in this manual, although for those whose disabilities require them to use a walking stick, among whom is numbered myself, there is still practical material in this manual.

Part I.

Chapter I of the drawing and holding the sword.

The sword will be drawn and *sloped* at four motions, according to the Cavalry Regulations.

In order to hold a sword well, the hilt must be flat in your hand, and the thumb stretched a little from the shell or cross guard[17], in line with the back[18]. When you guard or cut, keep a strong grasp of your sword; but on the contrary, when you are out of *measure*, keep it easy in your hand, that the muscles of your hand may not become stiff and weak.

---

[17] This contradicts the notion that this work is about the 'Scotch Broad Sword' which has neither at least in the basket hilted form that the name implies to a modern reader.

[18] See grip in the section on training.

Chapter II-of the figure of eight downwards and upwards.

The *scholar*, at *slope swords*, will be taught to *flourish* the figure of eight downwards, which is now called one and two[19], he will likewise *flourish* the figure of eight upwards, which is now called three and four[20]: - The use of these *flourishes* is to give freedom to the arm and wrist, likewise a notion of giving a good blow, and *throwing* the edge, which is the most essential part of a broadswordsman.

After the *scholar* is perfectly master of *flourishing*, he will return to the position of *slope swords*.

---

[19] See section on cuts starting on page 45.

[20] See section on cuts starting on page 45.

Chapter III-of the inside guard[21].

Being at *slope swords*, the right foot towards your adversary, eighteen inches from heel to heel[22], the left toe will turn outwards and cross the direction of the right; both knees easy and somewhat bent; the body leaning rather backwards, with the weight principally on the left leg[23], and the head upright; left arm forming a semi circle, height of the forehead, fingers easy, and the palm of the hand to the front; the sword arm well stretched, sword hilt at the height of the flank, thumb on the handle in line with the back of the sword, wrist turned inwards, that the cross guard of your sword cover the inside of the arm, the point of your sword at the height of your adversary's left eye, and a little inclined to your adversary's left, in order to secure your outside while on an inside guard.

The inside guard is the most used by fencers when meeting or advancing on each other, to begin the combat, and is much the handsomest attitude of a fencer[24].

---

[21] See figure 1.

[22] A stance a little wider than shoulder width.

[23] This will come as a surprise to sport fencers but is a standard stance in Eastern Martial Arts, e.g. the 'ko-kutsi-dach' of Karate.

[24] Handsome is here used in the context of elegance or gracefulness and betrays Mathewson's concern with promoting fencing as an art that is especially fit for gentlemen.

Figure 1 showing "the guard for the inside of the arm", after Mathewson (1805, plate 1).

Chapter IV-of the outside guard[25].

From the inside guard the right foot to be moved three inches to the right, the same time you *disengage* your sword to the outside of your adversary's, both knees a little bent, your left hand on the left hip, thumb in front, the point of your sword at the height of your adversary's right eye and inclining to his right, in order to secure your inside while on the outside guard, the weight of the body to be principally on the left leg, and upright, hilt at the height of the flank, and well balanced on your limbs, the wrist turned outwards[26], so that the cross guard of your sword covers the outside of the arm.

---

[25] The tierce of sport fencing although Mathewson uses tierce for his hanging guard.

[26] This increases the distance your adversary's sword is away from your body when swords are in contact and gives more power to your counter attacks.

Figure 2 showing "the guard for the outside of the arm", after Mathewson (1805, plate 2).

Chapter V-of the medium guard.

From the outside guard, the right foot to be *lunged* forward near four feet, in line with the left, the right knee well bent over the toe, left leg and thigh well stretched, both feet firm on the ground, left arm hanging easy down the left thigh, sword arm well stretched, hilt at the height of the chin, and the point directed at your adversary's breast, thumb in line with the back of the sword, and the nails rather upright as in the *carte thrust*, that you may according to circumstances *thrust carte inside* or *over the arms*-as the latter is most safe, and will sufficiently prevent your adversary from *return*ing a cut for your head or encroach on your distance.

Figure 3 showing 'the medium guard', after Mathewson ((1805, plate 3).

Chapter VI-of the hanging guard.

From the medium guard the right foot will be moved eighteen inches before the left, and three inches off the line, as on the outside guard, both knees a little bent, the left hand on the left hip, thumb in front, and firm on your limbs, sword arm well stretched, thumb directing the back of the sword, and the middle knuckles and edge upwards, divide your sword, by seeing your adversary three inches and a half from your hilt[27], under the *forte* of your blade, your point directed to your adversary's right, crossing your face a little with your blade; this guard is the best against a strong or inexperienced adversary, or for blows for the head, even by good fencers, you are likewise ready for parrying a *thrust*, as well as guarding a blow, and in a position for guarding and *return*ing either cut or *thrust*.

Figure 4 showing the 'hanging guard', after Mathewson (1805, plate 4).

---

[27] I.e. as per figures 4 and 18, this volume, raise your hand high enough so that you can look at your opponent under your hilt.

Chapter VII-of the four guards, left foot standing.

The *scholar* at *slope* swords,

Master[28] as words of command-"right foot forward to an inside guard", as in plate 1[29].

Master-"the right foot three inches to the right to an outside guard", as in plate 2[30].

Master- "the right foot will *lunge* forward to medium guard", as in plate 3[31].

Master- "the right foot to the right, three inches off the line, to a hanging guard", as in plate 4[32]- "and return to the inside guard":

After the *scholar* is instructed in the aforementioned guards, with the left foot on the ground he will be taught to *traverse* to the left and right, by moving his feet and changing his guards alternately, either the whole circle or part, so as to bring him to his ground.

---

[28] Mathewson is giving orders as if he were present and these words of command would normally be called by the master to co-ordinate a group's movements. To emphasise this point I have placed the commands in speech marks "".

[29] Figure 1 this volume.

[30] Figure 2 this volume.

[31] Figure 3 this volume.

[32] Figure 4 this volume.

Chapter VIII-of the four guards, traversing to the left and right.

The *scholar* at the inside guard:

Master as words of command[33] - "left *traverse*, left foot to the left to an outside guard.

Master – "right foot before the left to an inside guard".

Master "left foot to the left to a hanging guard".

Master "right foot before the left to a medium guard".

Master "right *traverse*, right foot to the right, to an outside guard".

Master "left foot behind the right, to an inside guard".

Master "right foot to the right, to hanging guard".

Master "left foot behind the right to medium guard".

The use of traversing is when you are on bad ground, in a corner, or the sun in your face, or when your adversary beats violently on you, that you are obliged to retreat, in place of which traversing is to be the more preferred, as you see your ground better, and not so apt to slip as in retreating.

---

[33] As per footnote 28.

Chapter IX-of the four guards, advancing and retreating.

The *scholars* at a medium guard.

Figure 5 medium guard, repeated from figure 3.

Master as words of command "advance on an outside guard".

Master "advance on an inside guard".

Master "advance on a hanging guard".

Master "advance on a medium guard".

Master "retreat on an outside guard".

Master "retreat on an inside guard".

Master "retreat on a hanging guard"[34].

Master "retreat on a medium guard".

Master "*slope* swords".

Breaking ground, as retreating or advancing, is likewise essential, as it doth by habit and custom instruct the *scholar* in his proper distance, and to *disengage* and change his guard as circumstances may require in

---

[34] Figure 4 this volume.

combat; to retreat one or two paces may at some times be necessary, but I would not recommend much retreating, as it encourages your adversary[35], and is a means of discouraging yourself, for it is not possible that a man being beaten back by his adversary can be in such good spirits as if he were advancing[36]. The *scholar* being at the inside guard, at a distance of eighteen inches from heel to heel[37], to advance, the right foot will move forward twelve inches, bringing the left after, making but one time, and keeping the distance of eighteen inches from heel to heel[38]. In retreating the left foot moves backwards twelve inches, bringing the right after, making but one time, keeping the distance of eighteen inches from heel to heel[39], by which you are always strong and firm on your limbs, prepared to receive your adversary, if he should think fit to make a fierce attack upon you[40]. The fore-mentioned lessons and guards I would recommend to be practised with flat wooden blades, in the form of the sword you mean to carry, as it will assist the *scholar* in holding his sword, and in receiving and giving blows with the edge[41].

---

[35] Indeed the posture recommended by Mathewson involving the weight mostly on the back leg seems designed to discourage such retreats.

[36] This is sometimes called the 'Spirit of the Steel' meaning that attack is better than defence since a sword is a weapon not a shield. Its usage here typifies the heavy cavalryman's thought processes and can be dangerous in fencing since it ignores the possibility that a more mobile opponent will retreat in order to attack you while you are off balance.

[37] A little wider than shoulder width is a good approximation.

[38] I.e. the feet are moved together by shuffling forward.

[39] I.e. the feet are moved together by shuffling backwards.

[40] I.e. keep your balance.

[41] For modern training purposes I would recommend these exercises are performed with the blade that will be used in *free play* always remembering to wear appropriate safety equipment, cf.

Chapter X-of throwing at the head and slipping the leg.

The *scholar* at the inside guard will move his right leg back, behind the left, and form his hanging guard, step forward with his right full three feet, and throw at his adversary's head; he will immediately recover with his right leg back, forming his hanging guard, and receive his adversary's cut for his head. These guards and cuts may be followed twenty or thirty times each, and the lesson to be practised until the *scholar* attains the perfect use of the hanging guard, and balances himself well on the left leg, and throws his cuts smartly with the edge.

Figure 6 showing an intermediate position in this move. The fencer on the left has drawn his right leg back and adopted the hanging guard. After Mathewson (1805, plate 5).

This is the most useful lesson in learning Broad Sword, as it gives action to the body to move forward and backwards as circumstances may require, and the leg being moved back in place of guarding with the sword, is allowed by the best fencers to be preferable.

Chapter XI-of the scholar's defensive.

Doubling for the head is done in the same manner as throwing and slipping the leg:-

The *scholar double*s one, two, three, and guards the cut for the outside of the arm, *return*s and pauses at an inside guard.

The *scholar double*s one, two, three, and guards a cut for the inside of the arm, pause.

The *scholar double*s one, two, three, and guards a cut for the outside of the thigh or leg[42], *return*s a blow at his adversary's head- guards his own head and leg[43]-returns to the inside guard and pause.

The *scholar double*s one, two, three, and guards a cut for the inside of the thigh or leg[44]-*return*s a blow at his adversary's head, guards his own head and leg[45], returns to an inside guard and pause.

The *scholar double*s one, two, three, and guards the cut for the inside of the body or face[46]; *return*s a blow at his adversary's head[47], guards his own head and leg[48], return to an inside guard, and pause.

---

[42] This guard was not illustrated by Mathewson therefore the reader is referred to training notes for this section, it is however essentially the posture of the right hand fencer in figure 9 but with the knuckles turned upwards so that the edge of the sword points outwards. It can be called a low outside guard.

[43] I.e. adopts the position of the left hand fencer in figure 6.

[44] The fencer on the right of figure 9 is in the correct guard, which may be called a low inside guard.

[45] See note 43.

[46] Figure 22, this volume, shows this which can also be called a high inside guard.

[47] This blow was apparently not taught in the official manual despite which it is known to have been widely used (Fletcher, 1999, 34). It is interesting to speculate whether or not unofficial manuals such as Mathewson's were responsible for its retention in use. It was however, also missing from the Naval Cutlass drill in its original form (MacGrath and Barton, 2002, 12). This may not be significant however, since the natural tendency of an aggressive fighter is to utilise just such a downwards vertical blow as may be seen by the necessity of Captain Broke of HMS Shannon to remind his men not to use this attack on their American adversaries due to the latter wearing helmets (Gilkerson, 1991, 8, 104).

[48] See note 45.

The use of the above *doublings* is to give freedom and action to the learner: also the *return* cuts is in general the best, and easiest to be got, as your adversary will most likely endeavour to get out of your reach, so that you are sure he cannot *return* before you recover and out of *measure*.

These *doublings* will be repeated as often as necessary, and as the learner improves in his lessons progressively.

Chapter XII-of the scholar's offensive.

The *master double*s one, two, three, and the *scholar* throws a cut downwards for the outside of his arm[49], and returns to an inside guard and pause:

The *master double*s one, two, three, and the *scholar* throws a cut downwards for the inside of his arm[50], and pause:

The *master double*s one, two, three, and the *scholar* throws a cut downwards for the outside of his thigh or leg[51], returning quickly to a hanging guard with your leg back, to guard a cut for the head[52]; *return* a cut at your adversary's head, and guard your own head; return to the inside guard[53] and pause.

The *master double*s one, two, three, and the *scholar* throws a cut downwards at the inside of the thigh or leg[54], return quickly to a hanging guard with your left leg back[55], to guard a cut for the head; *return* a cut at your adversary's head, and guard your own head[56]; return to the inside guard and pause.

The *master double*s one, two, three, and the *scholar* throws a cut sideways[57] at the inside of his body or face[58]; return quickly to a hanging

---

[49] Resulting in the position shown in figure 7, the scholar is on the left.

[50] The end point of this move is shown in figure 8; the scholar is on the right.

[51] The endpoint of this move is shown by the fencer on the right of figure 9. However, the reader should be advised that this figure actually seems to be thrusting for the knee and the cut should end with the knuckles of the hand facing upwards. The rest of the position is however correct.

[52] Figure 9 here does double duty with the fencer on the left indicating the posture to which the scholar returns after cutting for the leg.

[53] Figure 1.

[54] Ending in the exact position of the left hand fencer in figure 9 with the palm of the sword hand facing upwards.

[55] I.e. adopt the posture in figure 4.

[56] I.e. return to hanging guard as per figure 4.

[57] Movement 5 of figure 12.

guard with your leg back[59], to guard a cut for the head, *return* a cut at your adversary's head, and guard your own head;-return to the inside guard and pause.

These *doublings* will be progressively followed until the learner acquires quickness in throwing his cuts, and recovering, traversing, advancing and retreating, with ease.

Figure 7 showing 'the cut for the outside of the arm on an outside guard', after Mathewson (1805, plate 6).

---

[58] The endpoint of this move is as per the fencer on the left of figure ten although he is actually out of *measure* since his cut cannot reach his opponent.

[59] Here Mathewson neglects to mention which leg however figure 4's position appears likely.

Figure 8 showing 'the cut for the inside of the arm on an inside guard', after Mathewson (1805, plate 7).

Figure 9 showing 'the cut for the thigh or leg', after Mathewson (1805, plate 8).

Figure 10 showing 'the cut for the inside of the body or face on a strong inside guard', after Mathewson (1805, plate 9).

Chapter XII-of the salute[60].

When the *scholar* is perfect master of all his lessons defensive and offensive, with ease and freedom to himself, he will be taught to salute, before he *plays loose*, being at a regular distance from his adversary at *slope swords*, body straight and square to the front. He will *flourish* the figure eight downwards four times and step to the right, with the right foot full two feet, both arms stretched in line with the shoulder[61], palm of the hands to the front, the right foot back to the left, and *flourish* four times, and step with the right foot to the left; sword arm stretched to the left, and the left hand stretched out with the back of the hands to the front, and present your back rather to your adversary[62]; right foot back to left, *flourish* four times and step back with the right foot presenting your left flank to your adversary, seize your sword by the *forte* near the hilt, with the left hand, step forward with the right foot, at least four feet[63], and shake hands with your adversary, the sword being then in your left hand[64], bring the right foot back behind the left, seize the sword with right hand, and step forward with the right foot, and begin the combat.

---

[60] The movements of the salute should be performed simultaneously by both combatants.

[61] I.e. forming a cross shape.

[62] This action actually causes one to turn one's back to the adversary.

[63] I.e. a lunge.

[64] This aspect of the salute will surprise sport fencers who always shake with the off hand.

Chapter XIV-of playing loose.

Playing loose is a real combat with sticks in place of swords, where the combatants make use of every guard and cut they have learnt by lesson, and use every art in their power to deceive each other in the judgement of distance, guarding, *feint*ing, disarming, etc and the same exertion is made as fighting an enemy in time of war; and is a stage further to real fighting than the cavalry sword exercise than can be practised with swords, without endangering the parties practising[65]; therefore when the combatants have made the salute, they must take particular care to keep their proper distance and *measure*, and to oppose one another's guards, lest they should cut each other at the same time.

When you begin to make an *assault*, you must consider whether your adversary has a mind to attack you-for that purpose give a little ground and keep out of *measure*, until you can read his intention; do not let your eyes be fixed upon one part more than another, by which he can never judge what you have a mind to perform; never stretch out to your adversary[66], but rather keep a reserve in your body and arm[67], and assume a bold air[68], during all that you want to execute; I would always advise that your aim and mind seem unsettled in all your designs, that he may not guess them[69]; again it is decent and polite whenever you hit your adversary not to boast of it, the spectators are to be your judges; have ambition but no malice; such are the manners which every gentleman ought to adopt in an *assault*.

You must also take care that the distance of your guard be not too wide, for I would have you make your adversary think that you are out of

---

[65] As mentioned in the section on training, I am of the opinion that such play can best be practised with lightweight sabres and sport fencing equipment.

[66] This can lead to poor balance and allows your opponent to judge his *measure*.

[67] I.e. don't lean forward and keep the arm relaxed and slightly bent.

[68] Keeping the head up as if keeping eye contact works well here.

[69] I.e. don't telegraph your attacks by drawing back your arm but attack from whatever position you happen to be in at the time. This is something that the previous drills should have taught.

measure, which will oblige him to approach you[70]; if your distance is too large, loose your *measure*, your adversary believing you are too near him will certainly get further. Perhaps some will object to my not being firm, but custom will give me that firmness:- I have seen tall men, very good fencers, keeping a short guard and a good reserve backward[71], by which means he draws his adversary towards him, and is almost sure of his *return*[72]:- never attack your adversary but with prudence, and when you have hit him recover quickly, covering yourself with your sword, so that you may always act defensively[73]; if your adversary is not as much skilled as you, never attack him, for it is the prudence of a good fencer to bear the attack, and receive the adversary[74]:- you may not hit him so often, but at the same time your adversary will not have the satisfaction of touching you, as you do not expose yourself to his *return* cuts; there are many good fencers that are touched by others who are ignorant of the art, but this proceeds from their imprudence in always attacking- they are caught by hazard rather than by address and knowledge[75], which proves nothing in fencing is certain; but the art one employs renders it both agreeable and useful:- therefore by all means act on the defensive, taking care to guard well, and then you'll be almost sure to deliver the *return*. If you make an attack on a person not as skilful as yourself, never *return* to him but straight[76], which form swiftly, that is the best way not to spoil yourself in fencing bad *play*ers. When you are advancing on your adversary, take particular care not to divide your guard; I mean if you are on the inside guard cover well the inside, so you have nothing to fear but your outside, if you are on the outside guard, secure it well that

---

[70] Wide here means do not stretch your arm out towards your opponent when not actually attacking him.

[71] I.e. a bent arm.

[72] This is sometimes called 'magic distance' and is the distance at which your opponent cannot either dodge or parry your attack.

[73] Return to inside, outside or hanging guards.

[74] This very good piece of advice should perhaps be ignored by those who wish to authentically recreate the fencing style of hussars who should always be aggressive in accordance with General Lasalle's dictum that no hussar should outlive thirty (Johnson, 1999, 60).

[75] I.e. they are hit by accident.

[76] I.e. during your attack your sword should travel the shortest possible distance.

you have only the inside to defend; for it is incontestable, that if you keep a divided guard, you will have two sides to defend instead of one[77].

When you guard or cut, hold the sword firm in your hand; but on the contrary, when you are out of *measure* keep the sword easy in your hand, that you may be the stronger[78]. When you are in the act of guarding or cutting, do not let your adversary penetrate into your intention, and conjecture your guards; this you must effect by not minding his *disengage*s and false attacks, which are only snares to lead you astray, that he may throw in a cut[79].

---

[77] Prior to *loose* play this should be checked regularly by having the master, or training partner, place the edge of their sword against your own next to the hilt and then thrust in a straight line. If they hit you your guard is divided and needs to be corrected by moving your sword hand further from your body.

[78] I.e. relax your hand letting the little, ring and middle fingers rest lightly on the grip.

[79] This difficult skill requires the scholar to develop the nerve only to react to a real attack by his opponent and ignore all other actions.

Chapter XV- of how you are to act offensively.

If it is your intention on the first meeting to be on the offensive, feel his sword strong on the inside, *disengage* and throw a cut downwards for the outside of his arm[80]; next meeting a *feint* at the outside of his arm; throw at the inside of his face or body, sideways cutting one or five[81]; next meeting *feint* at the outside of his leg, if he throws at your head cover well, and throw in the cut a second time, and spring off under the hanging guard[82]; the *feint* is only to aggravate your adversary to throw at your head, which allows you with safety to throw in the cut;- if your adversary advances on a hanging guard, throw strong at his head in order to bring him higher with his guard, that you may have an opportunity of cutting four[83] under his hilt, which will bring you completely to your hanging guard. This cut is thrown under his point and will cross his arm from the elbow to the wrist; after battering his hanging guard to your mind, you may *traverse* one step to the left and throw upwards or downwards at the outside of his arm:- if your adversary advances on a high guard[84], on meeting throw a cut for the inside of his wrist, which is now called three[85]; in throwing the cut turn the middle knuckles well up that you may cut with the edge of the sword, as a touch with the flat would be of no effect to your adversary:- if your adversary advances on an inside guard, rather high, with the right knee bent, meet him looking over his head with your body straight and upright; throw at the inside of his knee, getting your body well back, and come nimbly to a hanging guard; if you find your adversary keeps his ground and does not retreat or *traverse*, follow him up and lay your blows in quick and strong, both in a straight line and likewise by traversing to your left, which will throw you on his flank and will give you decidedly the advantage.

---

[80] Once again Mathewson is assuming that his fencer will be at the inside guard. This move is performed by moving one's own sword under your opponent's and then cutting at the wrist.

[81] See section on cuts starting on page 45.

[82] Figure 4.

[83] See section on cuts starting on page 45.

[84] I.e. with the sword held so that the point is at shoulder height or higher.

[85] See section on cuts starting on page 45.

Chapter XVI- of how you are to act defensively.

If you mean to be on the defensive, and your adversary should throw at the outside of your arm, after forcing your inside guard, meet the cut with your outside guard, and *return* a cut for the outside of his arm; if you *traverse* one step to the left, your advantage will be the more sure; if your adversary *feints* at the outside of your arm in order to throw at the inside of your body or face, receive his cut on a strong inside guard, and *return* a cut to the right side of his face or neck, taking care to get out of *measure*[86]. If your adversary should *feint* at the outside of your leg, throw the cut for the wrist on his outside, with your left leg back, which will bring you to a proper hanging guard; if he throws in a second time, retreat and throw at his head or the outside of his leg; if your adversary should throw cut three at the inside of your wrist under your hilt, sink your hilt, and *return* the cut downwards at outside of his arm[87].

---

[86] I.e. move outside your opponent's distance.

[87] Experience suggests this to be the instinctive approach of most fencers to this situation and therefore neither specific instructions nor training to this effect are required.

Chapter XVII- of disarming.

When your adversary and you are advancing on each other, rather out of *measure*, through the counter of tierce, quick and strong, which will bring you to a hanging guard[88], and most likely the twist that you give will throw down the sword of your adversary[89], or if it should not be thrown from his hand it will give you an opening to throw in a cut, or that it may embarrass him and put him off his guard:- another way- when you are advancing on an inside guard, make sure of your adversary's sword[90], spring forward, closing up hilt to hilt[91], changing your left foot first and seize his sword arm with your left hand, and give him the left leg and he will most likely fall on his back[92]. Another way- if you are on the outside guard make sure of his sword[93], and run up hilt to hilt[94], and you may serve him as above. Another way- bear on his inside guard, step forward nimbly, seize his sword arm, or sword[95], with your left hand, and he may be served as in the last disarm[96]. If you find your adversary does not retreat or *traverse*, but keeps his ground, he is easily disarmed by any of the aforesaid disarms, or when on a hanging guard, if you think fit.

---

[88] Performed by moving from outside guard to hanging guard while making contact with your adversary's *feeble*.

[89] I.e. knock it out of the way so that it no longer directly threatens you nor is it in a position to intercept your attack.

[90] This performed by making contact with the forte of your sword and the forte of your opponent's and keeping this contact as you move forward.

[91] In sport fencing when the hilts touch a halt is called because it is impossible to make a good attack.

[92] I.e. trip him.

[93] As per note 90.

[94] As per note 91.

[95] As Mark Rector (2000, 293 n. 21) says in his translation of Talhoffer from his witnessing a demonstration of a sharp sword being gripped with a bare hand one must ensure that the sword is held firmly enough in order that the blade cannot be pulled through the hand or else severe lacerations will result. My personal recommendation is to seize the hilt or the pommel rather than the blade.

[96] I.e. trip him.

Chapter XVIII- of preventing disarms.

When your adversary and you are advancing on each other, keep your sword firm in your hand, and, after he has made an attempt to disarm you, throw cut four under his hilt[97]. Another way- when your adversary and you are advancing on each other, on an inside guard, and he should cross your sword in order to disarm you, give ground, and quit his sword, and receive him on a medium guard or *thrust*[98], or be ready to seize his sword arm with your left hand[99], as he will seize yours, if possible[100]. Another way- when your adversary and you are advancing on each other on an outside guard, and he should cross your sword in order to disarm you, give ground and quit his sword[101], and receive him on a medium guard as before[102]. Another way- be watchful that your adversary does not bear too much to the inside guard;- if you find that he is bearing very much[103], give ground, and quit his sword, and meet him on a medium guard or *thrust*[104].

---

[97] Nb this is only the counter to the first of Mathewson's listed disarms not to the trips and grabs.

[98] I.e. step backwards so that your swords are no longer touching and then perform the movements specified as per adopting the medium guard and thereby hit your opponent with either the edge or the point depending on distance one may choose just to thrust instead of performing the full medium guard movement. Nb 1 take care not run onto your opponent's point. Nb 2 if using the thrust remember to aim the point at your opponent before you move.

[99] This is an option if circumstances prevent one's retreat, but see note 95 above.

[100] For instance if previously your left hand has been injured this may not be possible.

[101] See note 98.

[102] See note 98.

[103] I.e. he is placing a lot of pressure on your sword while moving forward.

[104] See note 98.

Chapter XIX- of the beating of the sword.

The beating of the sword is performed by swiftly touching your adversary's blade with the point of your's[105], to try to baffle and put him out of order; if you find that he resists, *disengage* quickly, and throw in your cut[106]. Nothing deceives a bad *play*er more than such beating; for he is so embarrassed by them that he cannot afterwards shun the cut[107]; therefore, he that fences with a beginner or bad *play*er, has nothing to do but delude him by beatings, *feint*s, appels etc. An appel is a beat with the foot upon the ground, to render yourself firm, and to stagger and confuse your adversary.

---

[105] Do not take this literally; use the *feeble* of your sword not the actual point.

[106] The harder he pushes back the easier this will be.

[107] I.e. he will push back so hard that he moves too far out of position for him to respond to your cut.

Chapter XX- of the glizade.

The glizade is performed by dextrously making your sword slip along your adversary's blade[108], so that you may throw a cut at the right side of his head or neck[109]; or if, if he resists your force[110], *disengage*, and throw downwards at the outside of his arm; but take particular care to properly restrain and manage your body[111], so that you can measure and fore-judge what you are able to perform[112]. This is a very good attack, as it obliges your adversary to move either for guarding or cutting.

---

[108] I.e. make contact your forte to his *feeble* and move your sword along his to push it out of the way. Nb make sure you perform this at the same time as you perform your cut.

[109]

[110] I.e. he attempts to stop you pushing his blade aside by pushing back.

[111] I.e. keep your balance and don't lean onto his sword.

[112] I.e. once you have started remember your intention and do not get drawn into a pushing match.

Chapter XXI- of left-handed players.

To defend yourself from one that *play*s with the left hand, you must observe the same rules as with the right. The *play* at first will be a little more puzzling, as you are but seldom used to fence with them; it may nevertheless be necessary to do it now and; and *master*s ought to be attentive to accustom their *scholar*s early to it; that if they should meet with such adversaries, the situation of the sword should not seem strange to them on the one side than the other. Therefore a left-handed *play*er has no advantage over one that *play*s with the right; only the right-handed *play*ers are, in general, not so much accustomed to *play* with them.

Chapter XXII- of thrusting.

*Thrust*ing being peculiar to the small-sword fencer, I have not treated on that subject, except the medium guard which is a *thrust* on *carte*[113]; and I would recommend it to be used as little as possible[114], but when forced by your adversary, either on your credit[115] or absolutely in danger. Therefore, if gentlemen would wish to perfectly master the cut and *thrust*, I would recommend them to learn each separately- the broadsword with sticks, and the small sword with foils[116], to prevent disagreeable accidents that might happen by *thrust*ing with sticks, for no man can *play* freely the cut and *thrust* with sticks, without being in imminent danger[117]: therefore when a gentleman has learnt both, and should meet an adversary sword in hand, either in support of his honour or his life, there can be no doubt that he will have that confidence in himself to meet any kind of danger, and of course will take any advantage in cutting and *thrust*ing, when exposed to an open enemy; and I believe all good fencers will allow, that *thrust*ing is preferable to cutting.

---

[113] Interestingly the figure illustrating this, figure 3 this volume, appears to be carrying a variant on the light cavalry sabre the curved blade of which was regarded as less useful for thrusting.

[114] This remark is puzzling given Mathewson's association with the third dragoons who, as heavy cavalry, carried a sword intended to thrust (Carswell, 2003, 187-8), even if as designed it was not actually very good as a thrusting weapon due to having the wrong shaped point (Robson, 1996,21). One cannot help but wonder whether the troopers of this regiment use of their swords to cut that was complained at by Captain William Bragge at Villagarcia, 11th April 1812, (Fletcher, 1999, 38; Robson, 1996, 21) reflects the influence of Mathewson.

[115] I.e. fighting a duel over a point of honour.

[116] The modern equivalent of this advice would be to join a sport fencing club if one wishes to specialise in the use of the point.

[117] However, if the proper protective equipment is worn this is no longer an issue.

Chapter XXIII- of judgement.

There is nothing so necessary in fencing as judgement; it enables us to face all sorts of methods with advantage, to foresee the cuts or *thrust*s of an adversary, and to judge of his method of guarding, in order to elude them: it is by judgement alone that we are capable of arranging our guards, and directing our cuts and *thrust*s; therefore *master*s cannot too soon implant it in the minds of their *scholar*s, for they should never teach them a guard without telling them the proper method how to deceive it.

Nothing is so difficult in fencing as to know well the *measure* or distance, since there are no certain rules to determine and fix it- practice and justness of the eye must give you an idea of it; - it is a most essential point, and he who neglects to learn it, is often hit in an *assault*. To assure yourself of a right *measure*, you must pay attention to the length of the sword and the height of your adversary- therefore keep yourself out of distance until you know how far you can reach out. If you are engaged with a tall man, that keeps a good reserve in his arm and body[118], take great care not to get too near him, but be on the defensive, and guard his blows; also make your *return*s quick and straight[119].

---

[118] I.e. a bent arm which means he can reach further than it seems.

[119] Although Mathewson does not mention it at this point if one counter attacks to the arm then this nullifies many of the advantages the taller man possesses since, assuming rough parity in length of weapons, if he can hit your arm effectively you can also hit his.

PART II: Sword versus bayonet or spear

Of the superiority of the sword when exposed to an enemy armed with spear, pike or gun and bayonet; with plates of the most approved attitudes for Guarding, Parrying, *Return*ing etc.

Figure 11 after Mathewson's (1805, part II) plate 1 'of the inside guard, opposed to the charge of the gun and bayonet'.

Of the first plate.

Is a supposition of a combat between two men, the one armed with a gun and bayonet, and the other with a sword, representing them as looking out, or taking a view of each other's camp[120], the one a

---

[120] This would certainly be one of the duties of light cavalry; although it was apparently largely neglected in the official training manual (Fletcher, 1999, 32-3, 42 ff).

mounted dragoon, and the other an infantry soldier. The plate represents the dragoon's horse being shot by the infantry soldier, who advances with charged bayonet on the dragoon; the dragoon, after falling, gets clear of his horse, draws his sword, and meets him with confidence in the attitude of inside or *carte* guard.

Figure 12 after Mathewson's (1805, part II) plate 2 'of the hanging or tierce guard, opposed to the charge of a gun and bayonet'.

Of the second plate

This plate represents the combatants advancing on each other, at which time the dragoon changes from the inside guard to that of the hanging or low tierce guard, crossing his adversary's point, and feeling him strong, and waiting for his adversary's *lunge*.

Figure 13 after Mathewson's (1805, part II) plate 3 'of a low inside guard, opposed to the charge of a gun and bayonet'.

Of the third plate

This plate represents the infantry soldier after his *lunge*. When in the act of *lunging* the dragoon should change his guard to that of a low inside guard; in the execution of which the dragoon ought not to quit his adversary's weapon, but on receiving the *thrust*, he will reverse his sword hand downwards, which will completely deceive the infantry soldier[121].

---

[121] The movement here involves the dragoon pivoting his sword using the 'gun' as a fulcrum by moving his hand and arm between the positions shown in figures 12 and 13 while keeping his sword in contact with the 'gun'.

Figure 14 after Mathewson's (1805, part II) plate 4 'of the *return* or *carte*, after parrying the *lunge*'.

Of the fourth plate.

This plate represents both the combatants at the *lunge*. The dragoon, after he has parried his adversary, instantly *returns carte* within the arms, which finishes the combat[122]. The left hand might be used[123], but a quick *return* after the parry will sufficiently finish the business.

---

[122] The meaning of this should be clear enough from the plate. However, the swordsman should remember to aim the point before *lunging* or else he is likely to deliver an ineffectual bash rather than a decisive thrust.

[123] I.e. taking hold of his 'gun' with your off hand before stabbing him through the heart.

Swordsman's offensive.

If you think that your adversary does not mean to be forward in attacking you, as in the first and second plates[124], use the left hand either for the parry or grip[125], as you think will answer your purpose best, for the sooner you are past his point the safer you are: as the infantry charge with the bayonet is made with the left hand first, consequently he likewise *lunge*s with his left foot first, and not being practised to *lunge* and recover as fencers are, he cannot be firm when on his *lunge*, or able to parry or resist the *thrust* of a sword.

Swordsman's defensive.

In the second plate- if your adversary *disengage*s to make his *thrust* within the arms, form the counter in tierce, which will bring him to the same position as before, his weapon being so weighty that it is impossible he can *feint* or baffle you, for the longer he remains at charge the weaker he will be, whether it be a spear, pike, or gun and bayonet; the longer his weapon is, the weaker, and of course the easier parried. Though he uses both hands, yet the fencer with the sword is much stronger, and may parry any *thrust* that can be made at him with the above weapons. If you choose to parry with the hanging guard, you may it with safety, but your *return* is not so good as if you had parried with the low inside guard, for the deception is by no means so great; therefore he has nothing to fear from his half *thrust*s or *feint*s, if he makes use of the counter and circle parries of the small sword, which a very little practice will enable him to do[126].

---

[124] Figures 11 and 12.

[125] I.e. take hold of his weapon or push it aside with your left hand and move past the point in order to deliver your attack. Nb if pushing his weapon aside remember to move towards him to the left of his weapon as per figures 13 and 14, assuming the weapon is being held with the left hand forward, or else I guarantee you will be hit with the back end of said weapon as you move forward.

[126] Whether this, or indeed any of the moves shown in part II, is a practical move with the notoriously unbalanced 1788 and 1796 pattern heavy cavalry sabres that the third dragoons should have carried must remain questionable. This may be why Mathewson chose to illustrate these moves with a *spadroon* rather than a dragoon's sabre.

Part III: Training

Introduction

These suggestions are primarily intended for those who wish to use this work as a training manual in order to re-create a very specific style of sword *play*. They should only be taken as explanatory notes expanding upon areas of Mathewson's own work which may not be clear to the modern reader. As such they are intended to be used in conjunction with the transcribed text, including the explanatory footnotes, and reference should be made to both parts of this work in order to understand how to train in Mathewson's sabre. One should add that this is very much my own interpretation and that other interpretations are no doubt possible when working with a text over two hundred years old. Perhaps one should also mention my criteria for selection of supplementary illustrations. Where possible I have sourced these from other fencing manuals in order to demonstrate that Mathewson's ideas were not his alone but that his method was part of a western tradition that both predated and continued after him.

Equipment

Safety: the practise of any martial art is not without risk and therefore the proper safety equipment should always be worn, the exact nature of which is dependent on one's activity. If one is training in Mathewson's style as part of a western martial arts program then no partner practice should be undertaken without as a minimum a thick long sleeved jacket, ideally a sport fencing one, lightweight gloves of at least the thickness and padding suitable for sport sabre and a 'three weapon' fencing mask designed to receive hits from both epee and sabre. This mask should be worn even if *playing loose* with sticks since even these can inflict significant injury. Those studying this art for either theatrical display or re-enactment purposes will need to take advice from their group's guidelines and should in any case modify certain aspects such as dropping the point while in close proximity to a partner in order to avoid threatening the eyes and possibly lengthening the separation between fencers compared with the distances shown in Mathewson's plates.

Swords: these are a problem since no purpose built swords seem to exist that are entirely suitable and therefore compromises are required. The biggest problem is finding a useable blade that has a flat section to the back of the hilt enabling proper placement of the thumb rather than the wrap around grip required by hilts which do not possess this feature[127]. The best compromise I have found is to use the Hanwei Hutton Sabre which at an overall length of 37" and a blade length of 30" is of acceptable dimensions. Although the weight of 21 ounces is a little light[128] this is no bad thing since it encourages dextrous sword *play* and for this reason the use of lighter blades was recommended by Alfred Hutton (1991, 65) himself.

Grip

Since Mathewson's description of the grip is unclear I have included the following illustration, figure 15, to indicate what is required.

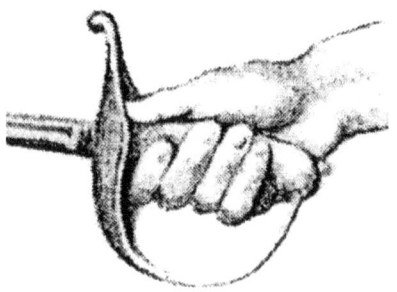

Figure 15 Hutton's (1889, 6 plate 1) demonstration of how to hold the sword.

---

[127] The rarity of these grips on 'highland' swords suggests that this grip is not particularly vital for this drill and any sword can be used and indeed the left hand fencers on figures 5 and 9 and the right hand fencer on figure 6 all seem to be using this wrap around grip. However, with practice it is possible to extend the thumb in the requisite manner even on swords without a flat back to the grip which is something artwork from the Vendel Period (Swanton, 1973, 204 figure 82c) suggests Europeans had been doing for at least a thousand years prior to Mathewson's writings.

[128] For comparison the 1796 heavy cavalry sword has a 35" blade and weighs 38 ounces (Robson, 1996, 19 figure 14) although often cut to 33" in order to improve the thrust's effectiveness (Robson, 1996, 21) while the light cavalry sword had a blade length of 32" to 33" (Robson, 1996, 18) and a weight of 34 ounces (Robson, 1996, 22). The 1786 infantry officer's *spadroon* at 32" blade length and 19 ½ ounces in weight (Robson, 1996, 144 figure 129) is possibly the closest match.

In accordance with Mathewson's own advice when out of distance from your opponent this grip should only be maintained when within *measure*, at other times the grip should be relaxed by only using the thumb and forefinger to maintain pressure on the sword. The middle, ring and little fingers applying pressure when required to quickly move the sword for an attack or to increase the strength of the grip when blocking your opponent's attack.

The figure eight

Since Mathewson did not include one I have felt it necessary to once again plunder the work of Alfred Hutton for a suitable illustration. If the *scholar* imagines himself to be facing the wheel[129] at *sloped sword* and then follows the arrows sequentially he will complete the figure eights both downwards and upwards, and also the two horizontal cuts. This exercise needs to be performed regularly in order to develop the necessary strength and flexibility in the wrist and in practice, following Le Marchant's (1796) drill they should be performed with the wrist only without bending the elbow.

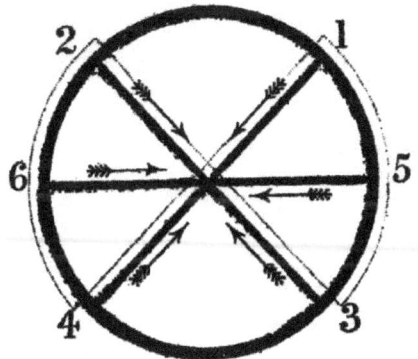

Figure 16 the figure eight, after Hutton (1891, 71 figure 20).

---

[129] As devised by Le Marchant this wheel would actually be painted on a wall and the scholar would follow the lines while making his cuts until they became instinctive (Fletcher, 1999, 34). For those without permanent training quarters a portable screen with this wheel painted on it that can be hung where you train is acceptable.

It is important to practice this exercise in two ways. The first involves paying attention to always keeping the cutting edge moving through the target to avoid wasting a good attack by landing a blow with the flat of the blade. This version of the exercise should therefore always be practiced at a speed slow enough to ensure this. The second way is to perform these motions as fast as one is able in order to develop the skill of rapidly changing direction which apart from enabling the development of confusing attacks from all directions very similar to the Sikh and Philippine fighting styles is also vital to develop effective parries where the absolute priority is to meet the incoming attack and then *riposte*. Therefore, although the same motions are involved never attempt to combine the two exercises but always be clear which you are practising.

Cuts:

One; start from the right and diagonally downwards from right to left.

Two; start from the left and cut diagonally downwards from left to right.

Three; start from the right and cut diagonally upwards from right to left.

Four; start from the left and cut diagonally upwards from left to right.

Five; starting from the right turn the sword hand so that the palm faces upwards and cut with a horizontal movement right to left.

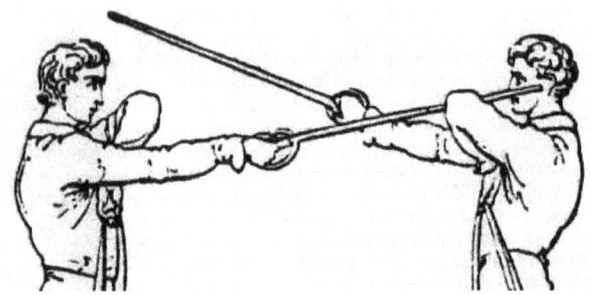

Figure 17 the 'fencer' on the left demonstrates the perfect end position for cut five, after Castle (1885, figure 130).

Six; starting from the left turn the sword arm so that the knuckles face upwards and cut with a horizontal motion left to right.

Seven; bring the sword straight downwards in a vertical motion. This was apparently not an approved cut by the army who restricted training to the first six cuts (Fletcher, 1999, 34) as per figure 12 above although it was used, and indeed has been called the most famous cut of the Peninsula War (Fletcher, 1999, 34), and is frequently referred to by Mathewson. Indeed it seems to have been the only attack used by some men to judge from Sergeant Ewart's account of his actions at Waterloo (Robson, 1996, 21).

Stances

Inside Guard

For this follow Mathewson's own instructions as repeated below.

Being at *slope swords*, the right foot towards your adversary, eighteen inches from heel to heel[130], the left toe will turn outwards and cross the direction of the right; both knees easy and somewhat bent; the body leaning rather backwards, with the weight principally on the left leg[131], and the head upright; left arm forming a semi circle, height of the forehead, fingers easy, and the palm of the hand to the front; the sword arm well stretched, sword hilt at the height of the flank, thumb on the handle in line with the back of the sword, wrist turned inwards, that the cross guard of your sword cover the inside of the arm, the point of your sword at the height of your adversary's left eye, and a little inclined to your adversary's left, in order to secure your outside while on an inside guard.

Outside Guard

This is essentially the same as the inside guard and is best formed by simply turning the hand so that the palm faces downwards and the cutting edge faces away from the body. The other differences that Mathewson introduces are a matter of taste not necessity. Thus it is unnecessary to move the right leg the required three inches in order to affect this guard. In a similar manner it is unnecessary to worry about pointing the sword at your adversary's right eye although the general principle is correct. Indeed I would suggest keeping your point threatening your opponents left eye will produce a better guard for the outside of your arm by keeping it further from your opponent's blade. However, if positioned as specified by Mathewson it will back it easier to defeat a cut to your own head by placing the sword in the perfect position to raise it into the hanging guard. This is a tactical point and is dependent on your adversary, if facing an aggressive opponent with a

---

[130] This should not be taken literally but regarded as an instruction to adopt a comfortable stance with feet slightly wider than shoulder width apart.

[131] This instruction will seem strange to those trained in sport fencing but will be familiar to those trained in Eastern styles such as Karate and Tae Kwon Do where it is called 'back stance'.

penchant for attacking the head pointing your sword at his right eye while in the outside guard may deter him from a reckless attack and if it does not will at least give you two options. Firstly to extend your arm and deliver a *stop thrust* to his face or secondly to raise the arm into the hanging guard in order to block his downward cut. If your opponent is more cautious then holding the sword arm a little wider and pointing at his left eye cuts down his options for a successful attack to your sword arm. Finally, Mathewson's adjustment of the position of the *off hand* may be safely ignored since there is no reason why the same position cannot be used for both these guards.

Medium guard

As advocated by Mathewson this is actually a *lunge* as per modern fencing although it should be noted that he regarded it as a *preparation*. This should be trained in as follows:

1) Lift the front foot off the ground

2) Straighten the back leg in order to propel the body forward without moving the back foot forward

3) Straighten the arm to deliver either a cut or a *thrust* while the body is moving forward.

Once this can be done naturally without stopping to analyse it all three stages should be performed at the same time. Although Mathewson seems to ignore stage three and the purists may like to do likewise I guarantee you will be hit regularly in sparring if you do so.

Hanging guard

Since Mathewson only illustrated this from the side the actual position is unclear and since it is used to guard against a downward cut to the head it is wise to correct this. Hence the figure below illustrating how to cover the body and head with the hanging guard.

Figure 18 illustrating the hanging guard from the front after Wise (1971, 247) who attributed it, incorrectly, to Mathewson (1805).

Hutton (1889, 8) recommended that a fencer return to this guard in order to cover his retreat and Mathewson himself frequently uses it such, cf chapters IX & X.

Chapter X

The point at which this exercise has reached a satisfactory standard is when the *scholar* can intercept his opponent's counter attack virtually every time. It is important when practising this technique to always make the initial attack real rather than to launch an attack that is too far away to hit your adversary, since this makes your adversary's *riposte* easier to parry it develops a false sense of security and the fencer who adopts this practice in training is fooling, and cheating, only himself.

Likewise the attacking part of the exercise can be judged a success when the attacks are landing properly so that the blades are contacting each other with their edges at right angles.

By way of further explanation the following figure is included in order to show the block from a different angle. However, the *scholar* should note that this is only applicable with a basket hilt. If using a more open hilt, e.g. the *spadroon* or the light cavalry sabres, the sword hand should be raised higher in order to intercept the cut on the *forte* of one's own blade rather than the hand. The position of the defender's *off hand* should also be noted; this was to defend the head in stick *play* and is not to be recommended in sword *play* although in a real fight a crippled hand would be preferable to a split skull.

Figure 19 illustrating the correct angle to receive a head cut in the hanging guard with a basket hilt, after Wise (1971, 247) who attributed it, incorrectly, to Mathewson (1805).

One must repeat Mathewson's own statement at this point and urge the *scholar* to practice this movement repeatedly.

Chapter XI

The constant reference to "guards his own head and leg" here means returning to the position adopted by the left hand fencer in figure , i.e. sword in hanging guard and right leg pulled backwards. The return to inside guard reinforces Mathewson's use of this as the basic *en garde* position in his style.

The cut to the head should be performed by turning the wrist and or elbow from whatever position it is currently in in order to strike downwards onto the top of your opponent's head with the edge of the blade.

The following positions were not included by Mathewson in his plates and have therefore been added from other sources

Figure 20 illustrating the guard for the outer thigh, after Le Marchant (1796, 80 plate 26).

One has included this guard since in the absence of any information to the contrary from Mathewson one has assumed he has followed Le Marchant, the official manual, as he did in chapter I were the draw and *slope* were to be taught "according to the Cavalry Regulations".

However, although for purity *scholars* may like to train in this guard it is not to be recommended while dismounted since it protects nothing below mid thigh. It is however, acceptable if the *scholar* also practices moving the right leg backwards to escape any blow coming in lower than this. This guard does however have one advantage in that a rapid attack to the adversary's face can be made by turning the wrist and raising the arm which seems to be what Mathewson intended.

Figure 21 Hutton (1889, plate XV) demonstrating the guard to the inside thigh or leg.

Figure 22 illustrating the correct position guarding against a cut for the inside of the body or face after Le Marchant (1796, plate 17).

Chapter XVII – disarms.

The first of these is self explanatory and the small commentary necessary can be found in footnote 88. However, the tripping moves need further explanation, although as someone with over twenty years experience at present in both wrestling and ju jitsu I would caution the reader not to bother attempting these takedowns since they require regular practice much more than striking with a weapon. One should also add a second cautionary note, if one is going to use any takedown check that one's training partner is competent at falling and that the surface is free of anything that might cause injury. To this end one presents the following figures, if the reader can understand them well enough to use them without further explanation then by all means incorporate them in your training, if not you are probably not familiar enough with grappling moves to use them and I would strongly recommend you stick to using the sword against your adversary.

Figure 23 one version of the trip, after Hutton (1892, plate 57). Note the additional use of the arm compared to Mathewson's simple trips.

Figure 24 demonstration of a reap, the fencer on the right has placed the body of his foot on his opponent's heel as his opponent has taken his weight off it in order to move away, if the fencer on the right pushes with his left leg towards his own right foot he will through his adversary. Those familiar with Japanese martial arts may know this as 'kosoto-gari', minor outer reap.

Figure 25 the fencer on the right has hooked his left leg behind his adversary's knee, if he pushes his opponent backwards while pulling his foot towards him his opponent will fall. This is the 'kosoto-gake', outer reap, of Japanese martial arts.

For added force this is best done by grasping your opponent's sword arm and striking him in the chest or face with the pommel of your own sword as per figure 26. Although this was not mentioned by Mathewson the pommel strike was recommended by Hutton (1891, 127-31) and is a particular favourite of mine hence its inclusion here.

Figure 26 showing use of the pommel strike and trip, after Salvator Fabris (1606) although one should note the right leg is being used here.

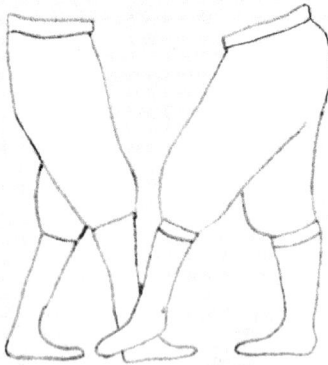

Figure 27 the fencer on the left is stepping forward while the fencer on the right has caught him with the side of his foot below the ankle bone. If he then sweeps his foot to his right his adversary will fall. This is called 'de-ashi-barai' by the Japanese, foot sweep.

The attacker can add extra force by either pulling his adversary's sword arm in the direction of the sweep and/or by using a pommel strike to the face or chest.

Glossary

Assault: series of fencing attacks.

Carte: the side of the body opposite the sword arm, i.e. the left if right handed. Mathewson also uses it as an alternative word for the inside guard.

Disengage: circular motion of the blade moving the sword around your opponent's weapon.

Double: quick time, here meaning a full speed attack.

En garde: the position adopted by a fencer at the start of a fight.

Feeble: the half of the sword blade nearest the point. It is so called because blocks made with this part are usually too feeble to work.

Feint: a movement that makes your opponent think you are going to attack him when you are not. It is used to elicit a response from the defender causing him to move his sword and leave himself open for the real attack.

Flourish: the continuous movement of the sword in a horizontal figure eight pattern in front of the body. It is so called because by some it is seen as involving unnecessary movement especially by comparison with the minimalist motions of modern sport sabre.

Forte: the half of a sword blade nearest to the hand. It is so called because any push against it can be strongly resisted. **This is the part of the sword all parries should be made with**.

Half-hanging guard: a hanging guard, qv, with the hand held low.

In fine: this is not a fencing term but is a Latin term approximating to the modern 'in short'.

Loose play: free sparring with sticks

Lunge: an attacking motion involving moving the front foot forward while keeping the back foot static. This is the basic attack in sport fencing.

Master: a term of respect for the fencing teacher analogous to calling a Karate instructor sensei. Unlike Karate however, the instructor is never directly addressed as such by his *scholars*.

Measure: if you are close enough to your opponent to both hit him and be hit by him then you are in measure. If you are further away you are out of measure.

Off hand: the hand that is not holding the sword.

Play: from at least the fifteenth century the Germans have described the use of weapons as fighting, fechten, while the French have called it play, la joue. In English the term varied by social standing and/or pretension, the working classes fought like their Germanic ancestors, the better off affected Norman-French ancestry and played with swords.

Preparation: any movement that places you in a position to launch an attack without actually doing so.

Return: alternative name for riposte.

Riposte: a counter attack following a successful parry.

St George's guard: this is the modern sabre guard of quinte and is often the first guard that beginners are taught in re-enactment where it is often simply called 'the head block'.

Figure 28 the St George's guard demonstrated by Hutton (1889, 69 plate 22).

Scholar: the name given to anyone who trains to improve their fencing technique.

Sloped sword: a resting position with the blade resting on the shoulder with the edge facing forward and the sword hand pushed slightly forward so that the whole rests at an angle. When used as a starting point for Mathewson's exercises the feet should be parallel.

Spadroon: a straight bladed single edged sword with a less enclosed hilt than a sabre.

Stop thrust: a counter offensive action whereby the defender attempts to prevent an attack hitting him by thrusting at the attacker in the hope that he can disable him before the attack lands. A word of warning on this technique, do not rely on it since it frequently results in both fencers being hit which if the *stop* hitter is being attacked by a downwards blow from a good quality sword will still inflict terrible injuries as shown by the death of John Ready at Lucknow who was killed in just such a manner despite having given his opponent a fatal thrust through the heart (Anon, 2006, 4). Indeed it was to guard against *scholars* relying on this technique in practice and then taking it into real combat with disastrous results that the conventions of precedence were devised in fencing.

Thrust: attempt to hit your opponent with the point of the blade.

Traverse: moving to the side.

References

Primary sources:

Capo Ferro, R (1610) *Gran Simulacro dell'Arte e dell'Uso della Scherma*, Siena, Italy.

Hutton, A (1891) *The Swordsman*, London.

Hutton, A (1889) *Cold Steel: A Practical Treatise on the Sabre*, W Clowes & Sons Ltd, London.

Koehler, GF (1798) *Remarks on the Cavalry; By the Prussian Major General of Hussars, Warnery*, London.

Le Marchant (1796) *Rules and Regulations for the Sword Exercise of the Cavalry*, War Office, London.

Mathewson, T (1805) *Fencing Familiarized: A New Treatise on the Art of the Scotch Broad Sword*, W Cowdrey, Bury-Street.

Thibault, G (1628) *Academie de l'Espee*, Leyden.

Secondary sources:

Anon (2006) *On the Use of the Cavalry Sword*, Ken Trotman Military Monographs 90, Godmanchester.

Brown, T (1997) *English Martial Arts*, Anglo-Saxon books, Hockwold-cum-Wilton.

Castle, E (1885) *Schools and Masters of Fence*, London.

Fletcher, I (1999) *Galloping At Everything: The British Cavalry in the Peninsula War and at Waterloo 1808-15*, Spellmount Ltd, Staplehurst.

Gilkerson, W (1991) *Boarders Away: With Steel-Edged Weapons and Polearms*, Andrew Mowbray Inc, Lincoln, Rhode Island, USA.

Hutton, A (1901) *The Sword and the Centuries: Or Old Sword Days and Old Sword Ways*, Grant Richards, London.

Hutton, A (1892) *Old Swordplay: The Systems Of Fence*, H Grevel and Co, London.

Johnson, D (1999) *Napoleon's Cavalry and its Leaders*, Spellmount Ltd, Staplehurst.

Carswell, AL (2003) Military weapons and their development 1750-1850, in Kaufman, MH (2003) *Musket-ball and Sabre Injuries from the First Half of the Nineteenth Century*, The Royal College of Surgeons of Edinburgh, Edinburgh, pp. 176-94.

McGrath, J and M Barton (2002) *Naval Cutlass Exercise*, The Royal Navy Amateur Fencing Association, Portsmouth.

Mileham, PJR (1983) *The Yeomanry*, The Yeomanry Association.

Owen, B (1990) *Welsh Militia and Volunteer Corps: The Glamorgan Regiments of Militia*, Palace Books Ltd, Caernarfon.

Rector, M (2000) *Medieval Combat: A Fifteenth Century Illustrated Manual of Swordfighting and Close-Quarter Combat*, Greenhill Books, London.

Reid, S (1995) *King George's Army 1740-1793: (2)*, Osprey, London.

Robson, B (1996) *Swords of the British Army: The Regulation Patterns, 1788 to 1914*, The National Army Museum, Chelsea.

Smitherman, PH (1967) *Uniforms of the Yeomanry Regiments 1783-1911*, Hugh Evelyn, London.

Swanton, MJ (1973) *The Spearheads of the Anglo-Saxon Settlements*, The Royal Archaeological Institute.

Wise, A (1971) *The History and Art of Personal Combat*, Hugh Evelyn Ltd, London.

Appendix I.

For completeness I have included Mathewson's own instructions for a Field and Parade Exercise en masse as used by the Manchester and Salford Independent Rifle Regiment[132] which may be of some interest to those studying this work for either re-enactment or theatrical purposes as opposed to those who wish to study a Western Martial Art.

Battalion drawn up at close order.

Draw swords, three motions.

From the right extend your files- a caution

March

Rear rank take open orders- a caution

March

Right prove distance of files

Slope swords

Front prove distance of files

Slope swords

Right and left files- a caution

Inwards face

Flourish and salute

Outside guard

---

[132] Quite what a rifle regiment was doing practicing mass sword drill Mathewson never explained since even the sergeants were, unlike the line regiments, banned from carrying swords until 1827 (Robson, 1996, 217) and since swords for other ranks in the infantry were abolished in 1768 (Reid, 1995, 11) it seems unlikely this was a drill from Mathewson's younger days. Three possibilities present themselves: only the officers actually performed this exercise, being a rifle regiment the sword bayonet was long enough to be used for this drill or being an independent unit they did things in a different manner to the regulars.

Medium guard

Hanging guard

Inside guard

Left *traverse*- a caution

Outside guard

Inside guard

Hanging guard

Medium guard

Right *traverse*- a caution

Outside guard

Inside guard

Hanging guard

Medium guard

Left files will retreat- a caution

Outside guard

Inside guard

Hanging guard

Medium guard

Right files will retreat- a caution

Outside guard

Inside guard

Hanging guard

Medium guard

Slope swords

Right and left files- a caution

Front

Flourish one and two[133]

Slope swords

Flourish three and four[134]

Slope swords

Left give point

Slope swords

Front give point[135]

Slope swords

Right give point[136]

Cuts five and six and return to *slope* swords

Right close your files- a caution

March

Return swords, three motions

Stand at ease.

---

[133] Cuts one and two performed together in a figure eight.

[134] Cuts three and four performed together in a figure eight.

[135] This is performed by having the "...troopers of the front rank raise their swords to the height of their faces, the arm extended in tierce, the point against the eyes of his enemy, and the hand a little turned, that the branch or guard of the sword may cover his own;" (Koehler, 1798, 46). This was the posture adopted for the charge while on horseback according to Koehler (1798, 46), although his accompanying illustrations show the swordarm bent as can be seen in figure 29.

[136] This is performed as per note 135 except that the face is first turned to the right, while keeping the body facing front and the sword arm is extended to the right.

Figure 29 showing the hand position for 'giving point' after Koehler (1798, plate 11).

On a historical note one should observe that the equipment shown in this illustration would not have conformed to regulations in 1798. The horseman appears to be a light dragoon however the weapon he is using is a long straight sword rather than the regulation curved one. Since Koehler's (1798, frontispiece) illustration of a 'Light Dragoon Officer' shows him carrying the regulation curved sabre one is at a loss to explain this unless it was either necessary for the artistic composition or light dragoons did indeed on occasion carry 'heavy cavalry' swords.

www.ingramcontent.com/pod-product-compliance
Lightning Source LLC
Chambersburg PA
CBHW031608040426
42452CB00006B/450